Politics of Media

Politics of Media

RANJITH THANKAPPAN

KALPAZ

ISBN: 978-93-5128-165-8

Price : ₹ 450

First Published, 2016

Published by

Kalpaz Publications
C-30, Satyawati Nagar,
Delhi – 110052
E-mail: kalpaz@hotmail.com
Ph.: 9212142040

Printed at: G. Print Process, Delhi

Cataloging in Publication Data—DK
Courtesy: D.K. Agencies (P) Ltd. <docinfo@dkagencies.com>

Thankappan, Ranjith, author.
Politics of media / by Ranjith Thankappan.
pages cm
Includes bibliographical references (pages).
ISBN 9789351281658

1. Mass media—Political aspects—India. 2. Mass media—Social aspects—India. I. Title.

DDC 302.230954 23

Contents

Acknowledgements

I sincerely thank all those who have encouraged me to compile the essays and bring it in the form of a book. It would not have been possible without the motivation of my friends to even imagine such a project.

I extend my heartfelt gratitude to Carmel Christy, Biju Raj, Sujith Parayil, Srinivas, Venkat Rao, Ratheesh Kumar and Sujith K. G.

I thank the Publisher and Editors for the kind support

- Ranjith

Foreword

The modern media are sources of power as well as of meaning–mediated meanings can have powerful social consequences. In a media-dominated society, all depend on communication media to portray and define those things that are outside the realm of one's own consciousness. Thus we "learn" about others through radio, television, movies, newspapers and magazines.

While writing the script of a feature film, TV show or a programme, the script writer (or journalist in the case of news) is constructing certain images. The script writer's own perception itself is marred by the popular beliefs that are actually constructed by the dominant thinking or discourse of that time. Media functions as an ideological apparatus or a cultural agent of power for the dominant discourse so as to maintain its hegemony over the public psyche. The representations in media, therefore, connote the ideological hegemony of the culturally dominant. These mediated cultural constructions have fairly good consumption in the heightened political sites of cultural nationalism that thrive on the essentialised perceptions of the traits such as religion, race, caste etc.

This collection of essays, published and unpublished, written over a period of time in the last decade, reflect the author's response to various social, political and cultural issues reflected in the mediated realities that define our present political culture. It ranges from media justice, media bias, scientific temperament, gendering culture and sexuality to cricket cultures.

I. Media and Society

1

Justice for Jessica: Seeking Social Justice in Media Activism

Justice for Jessica was not just a slogan, but an enigmatic campaign undertaken by metro-centred Indian media (both print and electronic) in 2006, eventually leading to the life imprisonment of the accused. Suddenly, media seems to be socially responsible and there is a cry for justice all around. And 'civil society' was exposed to a plethora of activisms harnessed by media and judiciary that tend to make a false belief that "justice" could be attained only through such hypes.

This essay is an attempt to problematise the liberal democratic facet of media and initiate the process of theorising it from a *Dalit*/Subaltern perspective. It focuses on the myth of media activism in the context of India's failed civil society and its monolithic, homogenous practices of constructing socio-cultural myths. A comparative analysis of media/judicial activisms with respect to 'upper' caste/class India and the lack of it with respect to *Dalit*/Subaltern India would led us to understand how problematic are the secular, modern and civil libertarian spaces in the Indian context. This has been attempted at the theoretical level by citing instances that define ideological positioning of the mainstream dominant media. Cases such as those of Jessica Lal have been cited in order to highlight and attempt to see the 'Other' side of these metro-middle class activisms.

The cultural parlance upon which these activisms place its ideological wings determines the nature of dominant media and its representations of Indian life. The term dominant media is used here not as technology or form but as an apparatus of culture, imagined historically as a nationalist organisation. Such an approach would not reduce media merely to 'form'; on the other hand, it places media as part of the historical, cultural, social and political realm of society. Here my interest is to understand media discourse and its cultural evolution in the modern context.

Media justice is a hypothetical term used to denote the contrived media space allotted for social groups to engage in public discourse. It is hypothetical in the sense that the term exists as a theoretical trope, tangibility of which is possible relatively at theoretical level. It is an accrued dominant narrative and its practice evolve as corollary to the ideological positioning of media as an agency of the culturally dominant.

Civil Society and Media

Civil society as a concept envisages a modern democratic society with citizen as a central figure and citizenship rights as a means to achieve the goal. Every modern society envisages an ideal civil society as gate keeper of its social consciousness. This ideal space provides a breathing ground for evolving and developing modern nations from the debris of traditional/feudal backwardness. It was in 1980s that the concept re-emerged in the public sphere debates in Europe and later spread to different parts of the world. The notion of civil society is today commonly identified with a non-statist, somewhat romanticised, set of institutions that stand for liberalism in the form of free market in the economic sphere and democracy in the political sphere (Dhanagare, 2001).The whole discourse on civil society therefore precipitates with the liberal intellectualism of the democratic public sphere. The visibility of this sphere is culminated in the media form and its imagined cultural sphere allows voices from different sections of the society to be heard.

The civil society should play a prominent role in shaping the concerns of this public sphere. The constructed media sphere becomes the 'coffee table' for the civil society. Ideally, the media should facilitate the process of democratisation by providing an arena for public debate and by reconstituting private citizens as a public body in the form of public opinion (Sridhara, 2006). Robin Jeffrey (2005) identifies the public sphere with that of the modern space provided by newspapers. He points out that "one can't have Habermas' public sphere without the presence of the newspaper." Both grow up together.

Media, by large encompasses the idea of an ideal public sphere, especially in highly political societies. However, a close examination of the same would bring forth the problematic terrain of these spheres. Rather than a 'public' sphere it limits to a space of caste and community where differing community voices demand the fair share of power. Thus, there is a possibility of problematising the imagined public sphere by introducing caste as analytical category in the Indian context.

Aravind Rajagopal in his book *Politics after Television* argues that Hindi language publications provide a much more potent site for Hindu majoritarian ideas. However, a critical analysis will reveal that English language press with its secular, rationalist image is no less a culprit. It could be argued that English language press is equally "Hinduised" (read Brahminical) in the very narrowest sense. Rajagopal's 'split-public' is imagined on the English/Vernacular language divide. But in a society divided on the basis of caste, sub-caste, religious, gender identities, 'the public' is a broken lot. As such, there could be number of 'split publics' vis-à-vis various identities which would in effect define the nature of the public/media sphere.

The secular and rational face of national media was exposed in the way the marginalised sections of the society and their issues were represented. The media representations of *Dalits, Adivasis,* OBCs/ Muslims in national media were in consonant with the majoritarian Hindu-Brahminical imaginations. The narratives have shown a hegemonic construction of these categories which in the large historical context end to demoralise and challenge the very existence of these groups in the national culture.

There is a belief among many who voice in the public sphere that civil society is live and capable of taking up issues pertaining to the marginalised sections of the society. Whenever Dalits/Adivsis/Muslims raise their voice politically, it has been branded as 'casteist', 'communal' and 'separatist'. Instead the civil society is assigned the role to "voice the voiceless". And as experienced, it never happened at any historical juncture. This anomaly is a result of mis-reading of civil society as a homogenous universal category which eventually led to romanticising of the concept.

Viewed within this framework of positivism one could end up believing that the 'universal' even if envisioned hegemonically, could not deter the basic tenets of the ideal. This is a wrong perception as 'universal' need not 'truly' represent the 'particular'. The 'social' can be better defined as part of 'particular' and therefore, might posses the potential to redefine the 'universal'. Both 'universal' and 'particular' co-exist and at times exchanges ideological lessons to define historical junctures. These are theoretical tropes, tangible in the temporality of the public sphere discourse.

Civil Society V/s *Dalit*/Subaltern

Civil society in the Indian conext is a myth. Otherwise, the tangible reality of its existence is predominantly a dominant narrative. It need not always voice the concerns of the 'split publics' living on the verge of caste, sub-caste, religious and gender identities. As such, its ideological concerns are very much 'upper' casteist. It is this Hindu 'upper' caste-ism that had defined Indian culture and therefore even civil society becomes an outcome of that imagination. Jessica and Priyadarshini may become a hot debate for this 'civil society', but it is a difficult preposition for those majorities falling on the other side of the caste/class order.

Khairlanji Dalit Massacre was a non-issue for the national media unless some Marathy local newspapers picked it up and sensationalised.

No candles burnt in front of India Gate, New Delhi for the unfortunate victims of Khairlanji. No celebrity vouched support for the victims. No newspapers television channel campaigned for them. No columnist expressed solidarity with the victims as seen in the case of anti-reservation/pro-Jessica-Priyadarshini media campaigns. These pre-planned campaigns were nothing less than political statements of the elite 'upper' caste minority dominating the cultural ethos of a civilisation.

However, those who lamented for the neglect of Khairlanji by national media also could not understand the logic behind the inherent media biases against Dalits. For example Mr. Sen who critiqued media's indifference to Khairlanji issue, however does not find the same for the media campaign against reservation. He views the latter as an instance of 'responsible media' and former that of 'irresponsibility'. He could not recognise that it is the same ideological framework that makes media support the anti-reservation campaigns and neglect Khairlanji. While anti-Reservation campaigns consume the prime time and space of national media, Dalit/Subalten concerns whether it be atrocities, human rights violations, success stories, daily life instances, death or birth, does not attract media in the same vein. These are non-issues for civil society and media.

Racism in the British Big Brother show was a debate for the British civil society and media. Indian media too shed crocodile tears for Shilpa Shetty's racist fate abroad. But where were these sympathizers and saviours of civil sense when Indian judiciary degraded Dalits/OBCs as 'non-meritorious', 'inefficient' and what not? Where were they when 'upper' caste students and teachers of IITs, IIMs, AIIMS, Central Universities and Private Colleges raised casteist slogans against major chunk of Indian population during the event-managed anti-reservation campaigns in Indian metros? Where gone their civic sense and modern ethos?

This was also evident in the famous Nithari Serial Killings of children and teenage girls at the city fringe of NOIDA in India. The elitist middle class who thronged with candles for Jessica and

Priyadarshini Matto did not come out of their houses in support of the parents and relatives whose sons and daughters were brutally murdered in a real life psycho thriller. The accused were a rich industrialist and his faithful servant. Right from the beginning the Police, vested with the power of enforcing law and order in the country, favoured the accused and victimised those who lost their dear and near. Newspapers have reported that the accused were once arrested against a complaint, but later released after receiving bribe.

In all the above mentioned instances, civil society and media showed less interest and its activism was non-existent. It never initiated a verbal/visual campaign for 'justice' as it did in the case of Jessica, Priyadarshini Matto and against Reservation policy. Nithari appeared as cover story with a sensational element of a thriller, but it never attained the dimension of a campaign. On the other hand, the controversial kidnapping and rescue of the son of Naresh Gupta, CEO of Adobe, a few months ago, got more attention from media and the state machinery. The political class offered support; state machinery lined up to serve and eventually justice gained. Media arranged virtual prayers for the boy's rescue through SMS opinion polls and scintillating accounts of the developments. Naresh Gupta thanked the "Indians" for their support: "I have never felt so helpless in life. Support from the police and administration helped save my son. *I requested low key media coverage earlier* as kidnappers would have taken undue advantage of our position. I got overwhelming support from everyone at my hour of crisis. But I am not a coward and won't change my lifestyle or flee India because of certain criminals. Life goes on. I am not bitter and still have hope in the system" (Italics mine).

CEO of Adobe has hope in the system. Moreover he is in a position to decide the density of news coverage. But the poor Nithari villagers are still not sure about the fate of their hope for 'justice'. Their hopes are shattered already by the system that constructed the 'world' for them. These victims belong to the lower rung of the society both class-wise and caste-wise. They were abused and victimised by the police whenever the question of lodging complaints were raised and even refused to lodge one. Media showed mercy to publish their photos in series; but they did not take up the issue as in the case of kidnapping of Adobe CEO's son. By and large, none attempted to initiate a debate or in-depth analysis of the social, cultural and political dimensions of the issue. They never bothered about the plight of the people living right under the nose of their avowed media consumers of NOIDA who speaks English and roam around in expensive cars. The people of Nithari may not have the same sale-ability as that of CEO of Adobe?! Therefore, Nithari end up as the story of cannibalism and nothing else. The social and cultural context that creates Nithari victims and their vulnerability to such 'cannibal' culture is undermined for the reason that none in power would like to debate it. Media being the cultural apparatus of the state, has shown the same apathy and indifference, and positioned against the majority of the population comprising of Dalits, Adivasis and OBCs.

On the other hand, these marginalised sections of society are ridiculed for the benefit of the dominant. Times of India's *India Poised campaign* imagine these as the burden on the elitist India. Times have every right to protect their 'elite India' for the simple reason that it is from the parasitic morality of those exploiters/oppressor's that these national media thrive in Indian media market. But they have no right to degrade and humiliate the toiling millions, whose culture and ethos make India alive. It would take years of internal democratisation exercise for the Brahminised national media to understand their life and culture.

Activisms of Elitism

An inclusive and responsible media would evolve over a period of time, but for that a democratic contour is a necessity. It is the duty of the civil society to create this space in any modern society (it is debatable whether India is modern or not). However in the Indian context where the historical ramifications of societal tension drawn on the lines of caste/sub-caste/religion get masked in the public sphere, civil society is a flawed construct. And as such activisms of this civil sphere tend to raise the concerns of only the dominant (read Brahminical).

Thus, media and judicial activisms act as a ploy to deceive the public conscience and create a false consciousness of an ethical society built on the pillars of media and judiciary. Call for justice therefore becomes 'activisms of elitism' that would only serve the vested interests of a few. These activisms of elitism are constructed on the caste lines of power and mask caste and its accrued narratives that jeopardise the growth and development of the society.

Instead of addressing the Caste Question, these fall back on the universal ideals imbibed from the west, at the same time limiting itself to the traditional ethos built on graded system of inequality perpetuated by caste. May be there is a need for more democratisation of media in order for it to offer "media justice" to accentuate the cause of the downtrodden. The media barons will have to address the issue of inadequacy of media space for the downtrodden either today or tomorrow. If they hesitate to face it now, the market will make them run for it tomorrow.

2

Reporting Imrana: Fortunes of Being a Muslim Woman

Dear Imrana, you are lucky to be born a woman that too a Muslim in 'secular' India!

Calling a Muslim woman 'lucky' against the backdrop in which her dignity is being challenged by a *fatwa* and its interpolations in the religious and socio-political dome has attained gargantuan dimensions, could out-rightly amount to condemnation on moral grounds alone. It is not a crime to be a Muslim and certainly not a sin to be born a woman. Yet the way media raked up the issue makes one wonder how lucky it to be a woman and a rape victim at the same breathe.

How did Indian media report Imrana? Does it handle the issue as a rape case or a chance to register its own latent anti-Muslim sentiments? Imrana's case stands testimony to the hegemonic ambivalence of Indian media. How more fortunate of these all-living women is Imrana, a 'lucky' dame from UP who landed herself in the worst of a controversy after being raped by her father-in-law! With her own honour as a woman at stake, now she has to collect herself to protect the edicts of one of the most powerful religions.

There is something fundamentally wrong with the way our mainstream media take up the issue. Usually the identity of 'rape victims' are not made public. There are clear-cut guidelines on how to report rape cases. Imrana's issue is a blatant violation of all such norms. It is not an isolated issue to look over by blaming the insensitivity of sensationalising by a solely market-driven Journalism. Imrana not figure alone in the list of luckiest women, but just dame of a dozen -from Mukhtaran Bai and Bilkis Banu to Regina.

No doubt, the pettiness and fragility of journalistic dispensations is what distinguishes out of these representations. Imrana's fate rekindles the medieval ethos, its acrimony that laboured hard to harness women in shackles for centuries together. It involves something crucial and socially and politically significant in general and to the women question in particular.

Imrana's case is akin to Big Dan's rape case, one of the most publicised rape cases in the history of US. On a March night in 1983 a Portuguese American woman was raped in Big Dan's Tavern in New Bedford by two men of Portuguese origin with the help of the bar assistants. The issue of rape, the unusual circumstances and brutality involved in it, were all submerged in the community identity of the victim and culprits. 'What happened' was forced to take the backseat and 'who are involved' and its overtones hit the headlines. The coverage of the issue pitted the victim against her own community and it drew wholehearted support from the public. It is one of the best instances of how mediated reality interfere and eventually replace the reality by nullifying the real issue. Often the victims and culprits alike for a virtual reality that submerge in its awakening the whole issue itself.

Imrana's 'luckiness' lies in the fact that she hails from a minority community. A mother of five, she has been used by the media to target the image of her community. That is why she got the strange bedfellows in Sangh Parivar; in the guise of supporting Imrana they indulged in Muslim-bashing and once again raised the demand for a Uniform Civil Code that would serve the ends of the reactionary Hindutwa agenda. It was not different with the women's groups also, they made much furore initially only to reclined into silence later.

Women who are not as lucky as Imrana are plenty– the Dalit and Adivasi women. When Hindu caste *Panchayats* issue orders (*Hindu fatwas*) and rape and parade them naked, that too at the behest of an age-old, outdated religious philosophy no single national daily questions it. The news is either buried in the corner or killed. Not even a single women's organisation comes out in open to condemn the heinous act.

The so called progressive Women's groups, led by 'upper' caste women, never consider the cause of Dalit women as theirs also. For them Darul Uloomas are barbaric, not the caste *Hindu panchayats* who run a parallel judicial system based on *Manusmriti*.

The caste heirarchy and oppression continue unabatedly with the support of the educated 'upper' caste Hindus. In every 60 hours a Dalit women is get raped in Rajasthan,where *Sati Mathas* (a Hindu Godess) are worshiped and religious conversion amount to crime. (may not a big news for a country where a woman is raped in every three minutes.) Dalit women can be raped; brutally murdered labeling as 'witches', for being outspoken or being courageous to disobey Hindu fanatism, for the 'sins' of her family members, for taking water from a public well, for dressing well etc. We Indians have discovered many ways to escape from realities and indulge in a revivalist reverie!

Imrana is lucky to live up to hear that women are second-class citizens, raped or not their dignity is of no value when weighed against that of a man. Whether it is fatwa or uniform civil code, it won't serve her cause since it evolve out of a patriarchal caste/religious consciousness that treat women as inferior and mere objects to meet men's lust. She is lucky to be left alone in the wilderness whilst the outcry for gender justice looms over the horizon of democratic India. Imrana is a victim of religion, community, gender, caste, class and media.

3

Ambedkar and the Secular Press

On the *Ambedkar Jayanthi* Day, while going through the pages of newspapers I came across a quite baffling facet of our secular Press—the blatant neglect of Ambedkar and the ideals he stood for throughout his life. It may not be quite baffling for those who navigate the secular tenets of our renowned Free Press. But for a student who is aware of the prominent role Ambedkar had played in the creation of 'modern India', it was indeed a shocking realisation.

Here the focus is on the English Press. For some reason unknown to me, there is a popular perception that English Press is 'secular'. The Regional Press, by and large, has been alleged to be 'biased', 'not objective' and denigrated for spreading communal hatred by manipulating the news. Unfortunately, this was proved correct after a thorough content analytical study of the Gujarati Press in the aftermath of Muslim genocide. The English Press was being hailed for safeguarding the journalistic ethics and secular tenets by providing an 'objective' and 'un-biased' account of what had happened on those scary days of the carnage.

Dr Babasaheb Ambedkar was a great scholar and charismatic leader of the freedom movement that the toiling millions of this country waged against the oppressive 'upper caste' legacy. His opinion was regarded essential in the matters relating to Indian polity. The national leaders including Gandhi had failed miserably in coping up with his ideological stand. Gandhi preferred to stand amidst the baggage of the marauding caste system, whereas Ambedkar foresaw an enlightened India worth living for the downtrodden that would represent the richness of our cultural diversity.

And how does Indian Press treat Ambedkar and his political portfolio? The National Press shared the same apathy that the nationalists showed towards Ambedkar. It neglected and at times misinterpreted his ideology. This was expected as Ambedkar stood in the path of the nationalists and opposed the 'upper' caste hegemony. Ambedkar's political treatise "What Congress and Gandhi Have Done to Untouchables" was a big blow to the Congress for it critiqued their uplifting project meant to entice the revolting Dalits. He expressed his strong resentments against the Congress and said, "We do not want any patronisation, we will fight for ourselves and our nation with our own daring, intelligence and abilities". He knew the indifferent attitude of the National Press towards Dalits and their cause. On the third conference of the All India Dalit Federation which was held in Mumbai on 8 May 1945, he remarked: "Dalit community is ignorant and simple-minded. They have no newspaper and yet there is such a large crowd".

Ambedkar's critique of Gandhi brought him the wrath of the National Press. During the days of Gandhi-Ambedkar dialogue which culminated in the Poona Pact, the Press tried to downplay Ambedkar's demands and projected Gandhi as saviour of Dalits. Ambedkar wrote articles in *Times of India* criticising Gandhi and this had evoked heavy censure from both the 'upper' castes and the secular nationalists.

Does this indifferent attitude of the Press change over more than half a century? Have the issues raised by Ambedkar resolved now? The answer is a big no. And yet Arun Shouries rule the roost. This was reflected in the cynical caption "Worshipping the True God" for a photo published in one of the national dailies showing Chief Minister of Andhra Pradesh Y S Rajashekhara Reddy garlanding Ambedkar statue on the *Ambedkar Jayanthi* Day. Did any of these journalists venture out to know the plight of the 'true worshippers' of Ambedkar in secular India?

The other day the Press carried news stories on the practice of untouchability in many parts of Andhra Pradesh (children being told by parents to observe untouchability in schools. Hail our secular education!!). Dalit students are being rusticated from Universities without proper enquiry; Dalit intelligentsia shown only in dim light; their 'merit' is being mocked at; and except the routine preaching of Dalit welfare activities the political significance of their cause is being derided. It's an endless saga of struggle.

The neglect of Ambedkar is the negation of the Dalit question. And this was unexpected of a secular Press that proclaims to be the formulators of 'secular public sphere' in the much casteist Indian society. Is there any hope left for the marginalised to expect a better deal from the Indian secular Press? The answer lies in how it perceives the Dalit question, i.e., the socio-economic development and the political representation of Dalits. For that Press should at first, tear away the sacred thread worn over their secular body text.

4

Politics of Obituaries

An obituary is a notice of the death of a person, usually published in a newspaper, written or commissioned by the newspaper (rather than written by relatives). It usually includes a short biography of the deceased. It is an announcement of the death of a person, giving details, which may include information about the deceased's origins, biographical data, survivors, religion and burial information.

Obituaries make interesting comments, though many a time confine to the ritualistic practice of journalistic writing. Obituaries are, by and large, personal/political statements to the core. It claims to be a since attempt to tell the 'true' story. But in effect, tends to denote the writer's interpretation of life and ideology that (they) tries to etch on the deceased. This essay attempts to revisit the media narratives of the demise of two prominent Dalit figures – K.R. Narayanan, the former President of India and Manyavar Kanshi Ramji, the Dalit leader and founder of the Bahujan Samaj Party (BSP), to see the constructions of the mediated image of the Dalit.

In the case of Kanshi Ram, the mere absence of a formal obituary results in imagining a 'political commentary' of his life appeared in *The Hindu* as the one. For the purpose of this essay, I include it in the category of 'Obituary, wherein the personal life of any person is political. Therefore, the political commentary assumes the position of a formal obituary, though not in the strict sense of its usage. Similarly, editorials written on K.R. Narayanan afer his demise have been treated as the same in the sense that the sub-texts of these narratives elicit obituarial sentiments.

The demise of former Indian President K. R. Narayanan on 9th November, 2005 attracted enough print space. It became the major editorial content and a discussion point in the public sphere, thanks to the flurry of news stories and column write-ups. In Kerala, from where K.R. Narayanan hails, some magasines came up with special editions dedicated to him. Almost all newspapers wrote editorials and tributes to the former President of the country.

These narratives situate Narayanan and his life in such a way as to prove a point ideologically over the discourse on caste and Dalit question. For example, *The Tribune*'s editorial (Nov. 10, 2005) constructs Narayanan as a logical argument that ridicules 'reservation'. It says, "at a time when the clamour for *reservation* in all categories of people, he [Narayanan] did not have any such crutch to lean on.." All the jargons of praise such as 'great son of India', 'nation will be proud of him', 'not a rubber-stamp President' etc. culminate at a point to argue and position it ideologically against the reservation policy.

The Statesman, on the other hand, addressed him as a 'Dalit India's dream child, fulfilling a Gandhian dream of total emancipation'. Gopalakrishna Gandhi also analyses Narayanan's life by placing him within a Gandhian understanding of Dalit emancipation, which for me is reductive and ahistoric. It is reductive in the sense that the narrative limits Dalit history to the corollary of nationalism and ahistoric as it makes invisible the struggles for freedom waged by Dalits in history.

K.R. Narayanan may not fit well into the traditional understanding of 'Dalit' and 'upliftment' logic. He is a success story. His success could be used as an argument for the need for more democratisation of the public spaces through affirmative action. Instead, the dominant media discourse places it within a Gandhian framework and argues against what Narayanan and his life meant for a Dalit.

Overall, the narratives of demise place K. R. Narayanan out of historical context in order to serve the vested interests of the caste Hindus, who oppose the democratisation of national resources. Therefore, the media discourse reinvents K. R. Narayanan as a 'caste weapon' against the Dalit question, that too, within the category 'Dalit'.

Gandhi, who opposed an Ambedkarite dream of modern democratic India where Dalits enjoy a fare share of political capital by means of separate electorates, becomes a rallying point for these narratives to construct 'Dalit life'. Dreams of Ambedkar and Ayyankali (Dalit leader of early 20th century Kerala) are non-issue; whereas Gandhi, who framed theoretical ploys to corner the Dalit question, is imagined as their savior by the dominant media discourse.

Though K. R. Narayanan is acclaimed as 'Citizen President', the Dalit politicians receive severe criticism from the national media, be it Ambedkar or Kanshi Ram. Kanshi Ram was the national leader of historical significance who passed away on 9th October 2006. After Ambedkar, he was the only Dalit political leader who could influence and transform Dalit life to a greater extent, especially in the political context of Uttar Pradesh. As pointed out by Chandrabhan Prasad, '...Kanshi Ram was a University of emancipation. He overturned Brahminism upside down... In less than two decades, he made UP Dalits walk with their heads high'.[1]

Vidya Bhushan Rawat in his 'Tribute to Kanshi Ram' has remarked that 'India's politics has grown through a radical change with Dalit becoming a mainstream political force; the one man who made it possible was Kanshi Ram. He worked diligently and religiously to develop a cadre who could bring the party to national mainstream and ultimately to the power in Uttar Pradesh.'[2]

However, a man of Kanshi Ram's stature is an insignificant presence for the national media. His visible political life and missions are made invisible by the media narratives. His opposition to Brahminism and the political dreamd of emancipation of Dalits make him an invisible presence in the media. Not only his death, but also the life and mission are neglected. As pointed out by Ravi Kumar, writer-politician from Tamil Nadu in his letter to the Reader's Editor of *The Hindu*, 'the news of the demise of Kanshi Ram was buried at the bottom of page 14...symbolic of the status Dalits are meant to enjoy in 'The Hindu social order'.

The Hindu published a 'long assessment of the phenomenon' called Kanshi Ram and wrote an editorial tribute the next day. The Hindu's correspondent Harish Khare's 'long assessment' of Kanshi Ram is an interesting piece. It showed how journalistic writing can be as harmful as, let us say, vicious caste violence. The piece was a routine half-hearted, politically loaded effort of an Indian Bagdikian Gatekeeper who was forced to pen down an obituary of his ideological opponent. Harish's assessment places Kanshi Ram in the 'caste cauldron' of political India.

Harish addresses Kanshi Ram as a 'caste politician' and denounces him by reducing the emergence of Bahujan voice in North Indian politics as a 'corollary of neo-liberal policies' and 'the rise of Hindutva politics'. He was not only ignores the Mandal Commission Report and its impact on initiating the democratisation of Indian politics, but also prefers to remain ignorant of the anti-caste struggles Dalits waged in history against the Brahminical hegemony.

It is from this historical continuity that Kanshi Ram created the Dalit rupture and emerges as a significant presence in Indian political culture. Moreover, 'caste politician' is a clichéd metaphor used cleverly by the political mainstream to denounce those who challenge or problematise caste domination. Harish Khare, the journalist while writing the piece has attributed his ideological insecurities upon Kanshi Ram, and frames him exactly the way Brahminical media demands. Christophe Jaffrelot could identify the 'silent revolution' taking place in post-Mandal India, but Harish Khare could not!

Kanshi Ram dreamt of a Dalit media to voice for Dalits. Though he could put Dalits on the national political map of post-colonial India, his attempt to form a Dalit media failed. Kanshi Ram represented the political aspirations of the emerging enlightened Dalits. And in the mainstream media discourse, this 'revolution' was mocked at, even denounced as 'casteist' and 'vote bank politics'.

The whole politics has been labeled as 'criminilised' and 'corrupt', as if corruption is a post-Mandal phenomenon. Dalit leaders became symbols of 'caste-ism' and were ridiculed as sources of political mimicry. Kanshi Ram and Mayavati form the central characters of the story where 'corruption' and 'caste' as aberrations form the central theme.

Perhaps, revolution whether silent or violent and assertions of the marginalised cannot be mediated, since the process of mainstreaming makes it imperative that the existing socio-cultural order is maintained forever. Therefore, the metaphorical representations symbolic of the caste violence against Dalits haunt even the obituarial narratives. The politics of obituaries, thus, shows the symbolic demise of a Dalit dream (of a Dalit media too) that Ambedakr and Kanshi Ram envisioned, and its hypothetical rise in the horizon of Dalit India.

References

1. See *The Pioneer*, 15th October, 2006.
2. See www.countercurrents.org/dalit-rawat101006.htm, 10th October 2006.

5

Gaddafi-Death the Gaze of Television

Do we struggle to find words to describe television today? It has become so popular that we know it like the delicious cusine on our dinner table. The new animal inside our homes- television- has changed even our daily eating habits. We cannot think of a moment in life without television. From the intimate moments of love and affection to dining together in the family, television has occupied our inner domains of pleasure.

It has transformed beyond a mere technological tool through which we open the window to the world and has become our inner self-our alter ego. The famous Marshal McLuhan dictum, 'medium is the message' has been extended to another level where the consumers of television visuals assumes to pose as the product (message) and the massage (the engaged targets).

Of late, the Libyan autocrat Colonel Gaddafi's murder provided the blood stained voyeuristic visual pleasure on television. It cannot be treated as any other televised event. On the contrary, it evokes the gaze of the dreadful reality peeping into our own conscience, but creating the hyper-reality in the form of a spectacle. It does not remain as mere historical reality, but affect the television viewer as a mediated tragic event. It makes us participate virtually in the event as a consumer of televised visuals. As Baudrillard has pointed out, it makes the television viewer participate in the event, but with the limited ambit of *ludic curiosity*.

Does the murder of Gaddafi remind us the Indians anything else? Post 9/11 offered not only the gaze of pain and pleasure, the pain of the tragic death of the deceased and pleasure of the momentous collapse of America imperialism. But it inaugurated yet another episode of American capitalistic and military might over the Middle East for controlling the oil resources and in the process, creating the Other in Islam through the ideology of islamophobia. The devious alliance of corporate capitalists, right wing fascists and American imperialism for virtually ruling the world through the control of the capital is the vicious political shift that had happened in the post-9/11 political world. And we are colluded and guided into this game of power through the path of hollow nationalism and islamophobia, which defines the way we claim to be secular and nationalist.

When we enthrall in the mediated death gaze, lest we forget to repent for the sins committed on our own neighbor from the minority communities. We are enslaved into the shameless reality of the everyday visualised gazes. We have transformed ourselves into American guns aiming at 'Islam as global Other' by imbibing the ideology of islamophobia; the mindsets that give moral justification for the violence of the state and right wing terror. Aren't we joining the right wing for bombing the innocent Palestinian children and civilians in Gaza? Aren't we the ones responsible for the years long torturing of innocent Muslim youth across the country?

Media becomes mere technocratic tool and globalised neo-liberal message in the post-colonial world. Saddam Husain, Bin Laden and Gaddafi are not mere names. These are metaphors for the violence unleashed by the global corporate and American imperialism.

There is hardly any distance we cover from the murder of Gaddafi to the everyday tortures meted out by the religious minorities and the marginalised. When memories die, propagandistic corporate agendas reborn as commonsense. And we realise in our half-sleeps that failures to remind people about it may lead to the brutal reality of the multitude of war. Global politics is written today with bloody hands, and not with peace. Television is its simulated visual signifier.

II. Caste, Gender and Science

6

The Invisible: Caste Exclusion and Dalits

"Strength will come only through a Bahujan cultural revolution which can be engineered only through our own media."—*Dalit Voice, May 1997.*

Dalit Voice declared it at the backdrop of a path-breaking decision by Kanshi Ram in the mid 90's to start his own media centre. What prompted Kanshi Ram was the apathy shown by Delhi journalists towards his political party and ideology. A ruckus between the party cadres of Bahujan Samaj Party (BSP) and reporters ended up in unmitigated outcry against BSP in the form of a series of newspaper stories in 1996.

The scene has not changed even in 2006. Kanshi Ram and BSP are still 'untouchables' for the national media. As pointed out by Ravi kumar, writer-politician from Tamil Nadu in his letter to Reader's Editor of *The Hindu,* the news of the demise of Kanshi Ram was buried at the bottom of page14…symbolic of the status Dalits are meant to enjoy in the "The Hindu social order."[1]In his reply Narayanan, the Reader's Editor of *The Hindu,* admitted that there "was an error of judgment which does happen in a newspaper at times. What really missed was a detailed obituary." He claimed that this 'error' has been "made up by the long assessment (Op-Ed page) of the phenomenon that Kanshi Ram was, and also an editorial."

However, this admission of error has not been communicated to scores of the readers of *The Hindu* till the moment I write this essay. The email reply of Narayanan and Ravikumar's letter of protest have been circulated and debated in the cyberspace. This essay is an attempt to place the whole debate in the larger historical context of political India and issues of cultural hegemony and media representations of Dalits.

Kanshi Ram is a leader of historical significance. After Baba Saheb Ambedkar he was the only Dalit political leader who could influence and transform Dalit life to a considerable extent. As rightly pointed out by Chandra Bhan Prasad, "He was a university of emancipation. He overturned Brahminism upside down…In less than two decades, Kanshi Ram made UP Dalits walk with their heads high."[2] Vidya Bhushan Rawat in his 'Tribute to Kanshi Ram' has remarked "That 'India's politics has grown through a radical change with Dalit becoming a mainstream political force, the one man who made it possible was Kanshi Ram. He worked diligently and religiously to develop a cadre who could bring the party to national mainstream and ultimately to the power in Uttar-Pradesh."[3]

A man of Kanshi Ram's stature is, though, an insignificant presence for national media. His visibility is made invisible by the media gatekeepers and the objective/factual/ impartial reporting falls into bigotry whenever a Dalit, Adivasi make their presence felt at the national mainstream. Not only the demise, but also the life and mission of Kanshi Ram was mis-represented. How can we expect the other way around when the Bagdikian gatekeeping[4] seems to be the dictum in the Brahmin-dominatednational media[5]?

The nature and density of the biased reporting of the national media had made Kenneth Cooper, the then Bureau Chief of *The Washington Post* in India wonder 'is there no Dalit journalist in this country?'. Kenneth Cooper who witnessed the BSP-Journalists row in Delhi and the 'unethical journalism' that spill the venom of caste-ism thereafter, wrote a piece in The Washington Post (1996) titled, 'India's Majority Lower Castes Are Minor Voice in Newspapers'. Only B. N. Uniyal of

The Pioneer responded positively to Kenneth's query and he started searching for Dalit journalists in national media He wrote: *"Suddenly, I realised that in all the thirty years I had worked as a journalist I had never met a fellow journalist who was a Dalit; no not one. And worse still was the thought that... it had never occurred to me that there was something so seriously amiss in the profession .."*[6]

Yet the Indian Fourth Estate went on with its hegemonic practices that inadvertently tend to stereotype the majority of the population without recourse to historic realities. As witnessed during the Anti-Mandal agitation of 90s and the recent anti-reservation streaks of the metro-centred 'upper' caste students of AIIMS, IITs and other professional colleges, national media always showed its true colour at all historic junctures. The national/varna media[7] never felt it necessary to head to the voice of the majority of the population fighting against the social order determined by Brahminic ideology. On the other hand they take on those who attempt to problematise the hegemonic deeds of the profession. Many among them are self-proclaimed "internationalists" who never want to become "casteist" by talking about Dalits[8]!

The question of representation of Dalits in media has a historical background. Ambedkar has pointed out towards the lack of media support for Dalits and their cause in umpteen numbers of occasions in history. He wrote: "Dalits have no press and the Congress press is closed to them. It is determined not to give them the slightest publicity. They cannot have their own press..."[9]

He contended that with a press in hand, it would have been possible to manufacture great men. And, "as there was no proper media for Dalits, there will not be any 'press-made' great men among the Dalits."[10] Right from the beginning of his political struggle against Brahminism, Ambedkar was marginalised to the fringes of political mainstream by the Congress press. Though, he could come out of the imageries constructed by the press, perhaps because of his mesmerising presence that could attract masses cutting across regional boundaries. It may be because of this realisation that Ambedkar once remarked: "Dalit community is ignorant and simple-minded and yet there is such a large crowd."[11]

The kind of response Ambedkar received from colonial and post-colonial national media reminds one of the poor coverage that renowned Black American spokesman Booker T. Washington got in the White press. Washington lamented that his successful speeches before large crowds that were normally expected to receive front-page attention would be relegated to the last page and given an inch or so of space. Instead, the front page would invariably be given to considerable reporting of a Black person involved in a minor criminal offence.[12]

Kanshi Ram realised the importance of owning media to compete with the corporatised national media. Though he succeeded in putting Dalit politics on national political map of post-colonial India, attempt to form Dalit Media failed for the simple reason that the caste-bound Indian social system is imagined in such a way that it naturally opposes the emergence of Dalit capitalism. Since post-colonial India has been constructed as a modern extension of Hindu social order wrapped in secular wardrobe, Dalits were imagined within the traditionalist Brahminical frameworks.

However, because of the Ambedkarite reservation policy that slowly democratised post-colonial socio-political India, a small number of Dalit middle class emerged. Although confined to the fringes of the existing affluent middle class, this newly formed 'layer of hope' spearheaded the "silent revolution" that radically changed the political equations. But at the media front, this revolution was mocked at and misinterpreted as 'casteist' and 'communal'. No, revolution cannot be mediated since the process of mainstreaming of media makes it imperative that the existing hegemonic social order be maintained forever. Our national media cannot be different and therefore we have Visible and Invisible Dalits a la carte of 'Hindu' India.

The Visible Dalit in post-colonial Indian media is a synonym for caste and the related aberrations. Media celebrates this Visible Dalit to the extent that everyone starts to believe that caste exists only for this category. The caste-dominated *varna* (old indian traditional classification of Human) narratives cleverly paint a 'secular' picture of their world. Visible Dalit has to contend with the blame of being 'casteist', even amidst their day-to-day struggles against caste and its modern practices.

Invisible Dalits also live in this country. They do dream, love, romance, dance, marry, make babies, use cell phones, read newspapers, watch television, listen radio and surf Internet. They too use television, DVD player, computer and go to PVR halls to watch Big B and Co assiduously re-imagining popular cultural lessons. They also know the spelling of Mass Communication and could function as better players in the long run. In fact many affluent Dalits are helping the corporate world boom by burning their brain. And yet, Dalits could make their presence visible in the national media whenever some caste atrocities occur. Dalit burnt to death; Dalit women raped and paraded naked; Dalits denied civic rights; Dalit students humiliated and harassed. Dalits always appear standing passively at the receiving end of development, atrocities or crimes. They are not allowed to break away from this framework. Else they become invisible.

The Kanshi Ram episode is a perfect example. The acclaimed article of Harish Khare, assessing the life of Kanshi Ram tells the story again in the same lines of 'Hindu' nationalistic imaginations. In his article, Harish labels Kanshi Ram as a "caste politician" and portrays Mayavati in such a way as to downplay the Dalit Identity Politics. He mis-reads the significance of the emergence of bahujan voice in North Indian politics. In his analysis neo-liberal policies and Advani's Rath Yatra were the basis of the political advent of Kanshi Ram. He not only omits the historic Mandal Commission Report and the demolition of Babri Masjid, but also prefers to remain ignorant of the freedom struggles waged by Dalits in history against Brahminical tyranny. For him Dalit equals caste and vice versa. Then, why does *The Hindu* which proclaims to be sympathetic with the Dalit cause choose Harish Khare to write on Kanshi Ram instead of any expert Dalit Intellectual as has been practiced in some other cases? A comparison of Harish's piece with that of Chandra Bhan Prasad and Vidya Bhushan Rawat will show us why it is so?

Kanshi Ram in Chandrabhan's or Rawat's writings are not 'casteist', but emerges as a visible champion for the cause of Dalits. Kanshi Ram as visible in Harish's writing is a brand label of 'caste-ism' and an accidental political invention. In other words Kanshi Ram's visibility is hegemonically linked with 'caste' and the wrong connotations of it. He is made 'invisible' by the media discourse and the constructed 'visibility' is accrued, which in turn is used to ideologically suppress the Dalit cause.

Chandra Bhan Prasad, the lone Dalit crusader is the only exception with his weekly column representing the Dalit world in bright colours contrary to the mainstream media discourse. The Dalit here is not 'casteist' and 'problematic', but a responsible citizen who thinks and dreams. He brings to light the beauty of cultural veracity of India that is less casteist and patriarchal.

It is the world of Invisible Dalit that would tell the true story of modern India. If at all India had changed over the years from a feudal/ vedic era of barbarism to a much advanced democratic world with the slightest hope for a downtrodden to dream of a better tomorrow, it is this Invisible Dalit's India that would show you the real colours. And unfortunately this India is invisible in national media. The media consumers are left with the lopsided stories from the upper echelons of the society, which echo barbaric feudal nostalgia even in its post-modern attire.

Invisible Dalits live with pride. Though in all walks of life attempts are made to humiliate them. It is their India that is invisible in Indian media. And it was this vary India that Kanshi Ram wanted to create with the help of Dalit Media. The question of representation thus attains the dimension of leading the process of nation-building and controlling political power. Unless and until the self proclaimed "universalists" tear away the sacred threads worn over the 'secular' body texts and helps the process of democratisation of national media, Invisible Dalits have to wait for another Kanshi Ram to be born for materialising the historic dream of a Dalit Media.

References

1. See Ravikumar, The Letter to The Hindu's Reader's Editor, www.thehoot.org
2. Prasad, Chandra Bhan, "Ode to Kanshi Ram" in Dalit Diary, The Pioneer, 15 Oct, 2006.
3. See "A tribute to Kanshi Ramji", http://www.countercurrents.org/dalit.htm, 10 Oct, 2006.
4. Bagdikian's gatekeeper admitted that he down played the Catholic Church whenever choices had to be made. See Jeffrey, Robin, India's Newspaper Revolution, p.170.
5. See CSDS study on national media, May 2006.
6. As quoted by Jeffrey, Robin in India's Newspaper Revolution, p.168.
7. This is the pet name given by Chandra Bhan Prasad, the only Dalit Columnist in the country to Indian media. See Dalit Dairy.
8. See Prasad, Chandra Bhan, "Castless Media" in Dalit Diary, The Pioneer, 8th October 2006.
9. B.R. Ambedkar, 'Plea to the Foreigner' from What Congress and Gandhi have done to the Untouchables.
10. *Ibid.*
11. Moon, Vasant, Dr Babasaheb Ambedkar in the national biography series published by NBS. p. 161.
12. Wilson II, Clint C. and Gutierrez, Felix (1985), Minorities and Media, p. 198.

7

Debating Pre-marital Sex: Gendering the Cultural Debate

The recent controversy over Tamil actress Khushboo's remarks on pre-marital sex has once again brought the category 'culture' to the centre stage of political debate, though its context seems rather inappropriate. Some would like to view the issue purely in terms of an individual's right to 'freedom of expression' and some one else, as a means to attain political goals by imaging oneself as the saviors of 'culture'. It is a sensitive issue insensitively taken up by some who imprudently prefer to get trapped in it.

The moral police of the country would prefer to script the entire episode at the behest of the fairer sex and place it in the lime light of the big cultural industry—media. There is an interesting prelude to this jinx. The entire saga of events began with a Tamil film director Thankar Bachan's vulgar remark on the morale of film actresses. Khushboo embarked upon the scene with Actresses Association taking a firm stand on the issue and the director had to apologise eventually for his nasty comment.

It is only later that Pattali Makkal Katchi (PMK) and Thirumalavan's Dalit Panther Party plunged into the scene supposedly to gain political mileage by taking up the issue in the interest of safeguarding 'Tamil culture'. The whole controversy took a new turn with actress Suhasini expressing solidarity with Khushboo and Tennis sensation Sania Mirza supporting the cause and getting the wrath of those who live with the moral calipers to gauge individual actions. The effigy of Sania Mirza was burnt in her home town Hyderabad by the activists of both Hindu and Muslim fundamentalist groups. The 'letter-to-the editor' column of some newspapers was flooded with "advices" to Sania. Thank God, they spared Narain Karthikeyan who was there along with Sania to show his concern for Khushboo. The dictum seems to be that Narain being a man has no 'moral' responsibility to religiously safeguard culture and is therefore free to express his views!

The moral police kept their mouths shut when the morale of actresses (are they not part of this so called culture?) was mocked at by a film director. As actor Charuhasan who has recently revealed in a Talk Show that he was the first person to be interviewed on 'pre-marital sex' and till this moment has not been convicted for "tarnishing Tamil culture". This is exactly the point that I would like to make here. Charuhasan has the right to freedom of expression and Khushboo has not. Narain Kartikeyan can talk about pre-marital sex and Sania Mirza can't. Why is it that always the women have to bear the brunt of culture? Why women are always targeted especially in all these cultural debates? And who has the authority to decide what is good or bad in culture? Above all, what is this culture that we are so much concerned about? Is culture static or dynamic? Or is it that some wants to see it static? And why? These are some of the questions that a gender sensitive mind can raise at this point of time.

Khushboo need not be a crusader of gender justice; she may not have shown the courage to question the patriarchal society and also the male dominated media industry. But she has got every right to express her opinion as a citizen and voice for the cause of women. It would be unwise to argue that 'Tamil women' are cultured and that the Tamil actresses are not. On the other hand, Khushboo's remark on pre-marital sex shows her maturity as an individual, though it may not be accepted in the hegemonic and Brahminical Indian culture.

The entry of Thirumalavan who is fighting for the cause of Dalits in rural Tamilnadu seems rather awkward, because the 'culture' he wishes to protect is the culture of his (Dalits/Adivasis/women) oppressor. It is an irony that Dalit Panthers who are haggling for a fair share of political power for the downtrodden, show this kind of insensitivity towards gender justice and by large to the question of cultural rights. An organisation like Dalit Panther is expected to side with Khushboo in the matters such as 'sexuality', in order to safeguard human/gender/cultural right. Instead they found Khushboo's observation on pre-marital sex (appeared in a magazine) offensive and launched stir against her. She was even forced into a murder case. There were more than — cases charged against her across the state.

However, the issue of gender and sexuality implicit in this 'debate on culture' should not be missed out and misguided towards the argumentative mishap of tradition/modernity dyad. That will lead us only to the cultural bandwagon of the fundamentalist Hindutva politics. The proclaimed ideals of Hindutva cultural nationalism won't serve the downtrodden. On the other hand, it is hell bound to suppress the uprising of the marginalised. Dalit leaders like Thirumalavan should realise the political debacle into which he is misguiding a "silent revolution" and be able to ideologically tackle it.

The entire episodic events have grown into a much needed debate on sexuality, although initially been reduced to the musings on women's chastity. Now it is the turn of those who were victimised for showing the courage to question the very hegemonic edifice of an imagined culture.

With much hue cry and the usual media hype over the issue, it has suddenly caught the attention of the youth. See how the youth icons Sania and Narain respond to it. This is a positive outcome of the whole conundrum. The need of the hour is to carry on this debate addressing the younger generation who are grown up enough to question culture and are the ones who can make sure that the society takes a giant leap forward. Society knew this and is afraid to let loose its control over the youth. That is why all these cultural debates—whether it is on pre-marital sex, dress code, mobile phones in colleges or love affairs—target the youth, precisely young women.

Gendering of these cultural debates will give the youth a chance to rethink on the prominent stanzas of tradition and culture, and come up with gender sensitive solutions. At the same time, one can't also forget the politics of globalisation operative in society and the changes it has brought forth in culture. This is the blind spot of globalisation that one would prefer to nudge away with. But it would also be unwise to think that one can enjoy the benefits on the one hand and keep away its most spiky trait—cultural change. With gender as framework, one can develop these abstract concerns to a coherent cultural approach and therefore to deconstruct some of the daunting socio-political musings.

8

Reclaiming Science and Technology

Science in India is an elitist fad. It gives legitimacy for not only 'merit' and 'efficiency', but also to the instrumental rationality for determining the where abouts of higher education in the country. The aura of science has engulfed the social conscience; from the agonising parents of a plus-2 student to academic intelligentsia and to the political class.

The arguments of 'meritocracy' that stem around science even unsettle other disciplines. For example, many academics use to lament that student's choice of science deprive social science research of "good people"! What implies is the legitimacy of science over other disciplines and the inherent intolerance of the modern *varna* of academia towards Dalit bahujan students.

And what happens to those Dalit bahujan students who manage to enter this world of 'elitism'? Are they able to co-exist with Science? To make it precise, how does one theorise the suicide death of a Dalit research scholar of IISC, Bangalore and the insurmountable silence of science community comprising of scientists, students, faculty and others involved in the production of science towards such recurring phenomenon.

One needs to look into the making of such imaginations and practice of caste atrocities in these educational institutions vis-à-vis the institutionalisation of science in the country. Such exercise becomes relevant in the light of the hegemonic appropriation of various scientific institutions by the dominant caste Hindus/brahmins.

Historically, science and technology was the traditional daily bread winner for Dalit bahujans. Leather technology, agriculture, medicine, carpentry, manufacturing arsenals, designing music instruments, dress making, painting, wine making, meat and fish production and preservation etc. were the exclusive inventions of the masses predominantly nurtured by Dalit bahujans. Political economy of the society was determined by these activities, though the priestly and ruling warrior castes capitalised on the productive outcomes in terms of material/cultural benefits. The philosophical backing for such a 'historical robbery' was provided by Hindu social order constructed on brahminical teachings.

Indian village industries thrived on the technological innovations of these productive castes. As these inventions arise out of the expertise of Dalit bahujans, the theoretical understanding of which was possibly inherent within. But, the colonial institutionalisation of Science put *shastra* as Science, and *shastra* when reduced to *veda,* the priestly brahmin castes became 'Scientists', so naturally! Technology was co-opted cleverly and reduced as the suffix of Science, once the offerings of global world brought 'cultural capital' for it. And these self-made 'Scientists' began safe-guarding their privileged institutions of both science and caste, as if performing their *dharma*.

Science thus assay forth in the caste order as mere brahminical rhetoric. The 'theory' of the masses was stolen and traditionally accrued as intellectual property of the priestly castes. And when post-colonial India carved out her scientific educational institutions on the footsteps of colonial masters, the science and technology of the masses were neglected. Science was kept away from the masses, negating an opportunity for them to theoretically contemplate and compete with western technological offerings.

Renowned Scientific Institutions, Medical and Engineering Colleges, IITs, IIITs, AIIMS, University Science Departments etc.

which establish science education in the country, witness institutionalised caste crimes committed gruesomely against Dalit bahujan sisters and brothers. Modern institutionalis ation of science and technology has deprived Dalit bahujans of the cultural capital, it provides in the globalised world.

Unfortunately, the polity determined by post-colonial *shudra* who rose to the political power centres as a historical rupture catalyzed by Mandalisation, could not resist this ploy effectively. The anti-brahmin base of *shudras* possesses an 'inherent' inability to counter the brahminical caste-ism looming alarmingly in the habitus of science and technology.

What is the result of such brahminical appropriation of science? Even today, superstitions rule the roost with tacit religious approval. Any *Baba* can make Indians kill their sons and daughters; drink poisonous water, worship milk consuming idols with bleeding eyes; cricket matches co-prophesied by astrologers and numerologists; life fashioned by Techno *Gurus* and 'God-men'; relationships decided on caste signs; 'honour killings' to safeguard caste status; *pujas* performed before scientific missions; government offices apparently turned into caste castles. 21st century India lives with these marks of reactionary ethics.

We terribly lack scientific temperament and it should make us contemplate on the plight of our science education. Absence of reasoning, logical thinking and socio-political outlook of our future practitioners of science is a real concern. Harnessing traditional retrograde ideologies of brahminism in the name of science cause pedagogical chaos as it produce only a generation devoid of any social concern and ***'true'*** scientific temperament.

Democratisation of these institutions should be given priority in order to reclaim the lost 'science and technology' of the masses. Scientific temperament of the people would be the base upon which new India could be built. Caste is the tool used for building societal power equations; it would also serve the very purpose of turning it upside down while constituting new equations of power for an egalitarian scientific world.

9

Casteing the Indian

Of late, Amitabh Bhachchan in his inimical style has blogged out to become the self-appointed member of the caste called 'Indian'. In the similar fashion, the popular academics of the ilk Vivek Dhareswar, Nandini Sundar et al., have polemically put forward their case against including caste in the census 2010.

An array of academic gentry follows suit as usual. And in popular culture, apart from Big B, there comes another Big B of the 'B'-dominated national media- Barkha Dutt- singing the same old tune, the 'caste of the Indian' fuming in their blood, masked as 'secular' suiting the liberal democratic social attire of post-colonial societies.

I would rather disagree with all these positions with due respect and put forward a context of lived experience to argue in favour of caste census, and of course in the same polemical vein.

Prakash Jha's Rajneeti is a failed blockbuster movie, so is Mani Ratnam's Raavan. This is not in the sense of box office responses, but its naiveté was as pompous as it could hardly capture the socio-political reality of the cultural terrain it was struggling to portray.

But a counter question would be, 'can any Jha or Mani ever capture it'? Kindly excuse me for being so blatantly casteist.

Huh, after all, what we could read between the lines or see through the visuals of all these hindu secular humanist way of cultural representation of our social realities tend to be etched out of this hidden reality- caste!

No wonder in a country fetished out of the offerings of colonial modernity, what nationalism and its borrowed model of developmental modernity and secular credentials could offer was nothing but a hypocritical dual life.

So we have to bear with Rajneetis and Raavans, so as with the hypocritical dual role of the new caste habitus of 'the Indian', at least for the time being.

The context that I am referring to has got many folds. Let me unfold one: that of a house hunt in a metro-city. After moving to a new city – Hyderabad - I was accompanying my friend in search of a house on rent.

Getting inspired from the chattering class of the ilk of Mr Bachchan, we were usurping in the glory of the newly imagined garb of the Indian. Can any one live that smart any longer in a country like India?

So we were also expecting the same chattering class tear apart the notion of the Indian in shear seething frustration. And the moments passed. The usual queries on surname or full name, region, vegetarianism, religion, caste.. None!

For a while we thought whether the country has changed after Big B or not? And then came the deciding moment of the century.

A retired scientist from National Institute of Nutrition and seemingly belong to the same chattering class of Big B to whom my friend talked over phone.

First question, after hearing that he is from Kerala; "So you must be a Nair?"

My friend said; "No."

Second Question: "So, an Ezhava?"

My Friend; "No."

After a pose; "Are you a vegetarian?"

My Friend; "No"

Again pose. And then came the crucial deciding comment; "I have no problem but we prefer to give our house to vegetarians, you know!"

A case indeed worth mentioning in the country of 'the Indian'. We do not get offended with such remarks, do we? It is routine for us.

Another such routine incident had unfolded years back when I was working in a media firm in Kerala. One of my colleagues was always curious to know my full name. When I told what my name was, he repeatedly asked what my initial means.

In kerala, these are some of the covert methods employed to find out someone's caste. Similar thing happened when I shifted to Delhi and joined a Central University. One lady in the centre got curious again about my 'initial'. When I told her that it is my father's name and not my caste, one should have seen her face fade as if unable to discover something precious or so.

I can go on narrating such instances, but our chattering class of 'Indians' will never be satisfied. They feel, enumerating caste will divide us and it is methodologically difficult to get the exact caste composition and their fear of numbers disguised as the call for unity and all other tall claims go on and so forth.

And remember, it is the same meritorious clan of the Indians who demanded data that too census data about the population of OBCs in the country a few years back!

Whether your caste enumerator asks or not, WE THE INDIANS have been asking the question of caste to each and every individual we meet on our daily life.

We have been doing the enumeration of caste in various lived contexts in order to make a match, join a peer group, shortlist a candidate, employ a professional, vote for a party, assess a student, while filing an 'objective' journalistic report and writing a theoretical treatise and so on.

The enumeration work has been on since ages. Now let us make it official and let Indian Government do it for us. And let us not forget to count 'the Indian' and of course, the Brahman as well. Let us help them get out of their fear of numbers.

Let me conclude with a piece referred by Partha Chaterjee (1999) while delineating the connections of communities and nation in his work Nation and its fragments.

The piece is a context taken from Bankim's Kamalakanta. The context is where Kamalakanta has been called in as a witness in court in a case of petty theft.

The lawyer then asked him, "What *jati* (caste) are you?"

K: Am I a *jati?* (caste)

LAWYER: What jati do you belong to?

K: To the Hindu *jati* (caste).

LAWYER: Oh, come now! What *varna?* (class)

K: A very very dark *varna* (Class).

LAWYER: What the hell is going on here! Why did I have to call a witness like this? I say, do you have *jati?* (caste)

K: Who can take it from me?

The magistrate saw that the lawyer was getting nowhere. He said, "You know there are many kinds of jati among Hindus, such as Brahman, Kayastha, Kaibarta. Which one of these *jati* do you belong to?"

K: My lord! All this is the lawyer's fault! He can see I have the sacred thread around my neck. I have said my name is *Chakravarti*. How am I to know that he will not be able to deduce that I am a *Brahman*?

The magistrate wrote, “Caste: Brahman.”

What ‘the Indian’, in their inimical covert style like Kamalakanta try to tell us is this, “Do you want us to tell. Can’t you see what caste we belong to?”

Let us not hesitate.

Go on and count THEM too.

10

Re-thinking Media Education

The UNESCO exercise to develop model curricula for developing countries has paid off. Now the country witnesses similar exercises across media schools and departments, but sadly at the cost of academic quality and rigor. The amount of money poured into this "education business" can be gauged by the number of self-born media/communication schools both in private and public sectors. Even, the 'hidden agenda' behind some of the newly established media schools in the country seems to be limited to generate revenue only. Media education has degraded to the extent that even those in public funded universities consider it as a money-vending machine.

In response to the UNESCO exercise, Prof Eapen, one of the pioneers of media education in the country has categorically pointed towards the need to re-visit the ethical and pedagogical aspects of today's much sought after profession.[1] This article could be read as a continuation of Prof Eapen's piece and more so, a brief take on media education in Indian context.

Social Relevance

Journalism and Mass Communication has developed into a full-fledged inter-disciplinary field of study in consonant with the socio-cultural changes brought forth by the process of mediations happening in industrialised and industrialising societies. This has inadvertently resulted in tremendous exponential growth in the number of media schools all over the world.

As the world has become more and more "mediated", the atomised realm of modern human beings and the socio-cultural impact upon its imagined terrains (say for example nation)[2] created multiple focal points to address social reality and the mass response, as suggested by media impact studies point towards a role-reversal. With the citizen sitting at the helm as the pro-generator of meaning, techno-deterministic positivism of development communication has already co-opted the mission. The initiatives such as community radio will be heard more today, but will have least social impact as its revenue model being tilted largely towards the donor NGOs.

As the cultural realm takes over public consumption patterns of media, the new age consumer has grown into a self-drawn media house of bloggers while social networking sites profile your public life. If one cares least about such cultural transformations vis-à-vis the mediated virtual reality, and yet wants to engage with the pedagogic exercise by a mere "copy-pasting" from the West, the coming generations will reject you out-rightly. Sadly, without referring any particular case (as there are so many such cases available) this is what could be termed a decent description of the pedagogic exercises undertaken in many media departments/schools in the country. In this context, I would like to argue that the responsibility of any media school lies in not to limit its intellectual horizon to the demands of media industry, but also to make academic interventions that would address the nuances of the cultural processes of media and mediation.

Whether journalists are born or created is an age old debate. The old school will vouch for the first and post-modern, the latter. A wider look at the institutionalisation of journalism at the initial stages may strengthen the argument for born journalists. But one should critically look at this ' holy birth of journalists'. I would rather argue that it has arisen in response to certain socio-cultural discourses at historical junctures. In the emergent global scenario, where not only skills, but a keen understanding of various social, political, and cultural aspects vis-à-vis regional contextualisation forms an inextricable part of any discipline, media education needs a revamp keeping in mind the capitalist emergence of journalism as profession. And as such, the UNESCO's 'Model Curricula for Journalism Education for Developing Countries and Emerging Democracies' was a path breaking effort, indeed.

In the Indian context, Journalism as an institution has developed along with the formation of 'public sphere' during colonial period. Contrary to the nationalist imagination, various asserting caste, and community groups have played a significant role in its inception. It has grown over the years from a colonial community enterprise to capitalist corporate business. Today, the market defines 'Fourth Estate' vertically where feudal/colonial ethos preserved in a new garb.

In the West, corporate aristocracy has been balanced by drawing a horizontal tangential in the form of 'affirmative action', both as a strategy and part of pedagogy. This shows the perceived levels of social understanding of western media corporate, thanks to various social movements and ideals of Enlightenment. Therefore, there exists a relatively 'progressive' outlook that had benefited media education as well.[3]

The ascriptive nature of education traditionally prevailing in Indian society has crippled the growth of our society. As education became preserve of the few, any revolt in the Indian context were counter-poised with the educational hegemony. Education was the emancipatory project for the toiling millions. Social movements that brought forth 'Renaissance' in various parts of the country focused on the issue of 'education for all' which eventually led to social mobility and change.

The visionaries of independent India too adopted the philosophy of educating the masses. However, because of the perpetuation and superimposition of a feudal social order onto the modern context, its imagined spheres remain predominantly elitist. Thus slogans have been taken over by statist interventions where "reaching the un-reached" become a mere rhetoric to create yet another elitist hurdle at the realm of education and culture.

The communitarian (in the sense of community) enterprise of education taking over social concern through commercialisation has been the silent, but sudden offshoot of the response from the elitist paving the path for the growth of self-financing private educational institutions all over the country. Though these commercial educational institutions used universal jargons to 'sell' education, its logic remain the same as that in medieval feudal era. And as a result of it, the concern shown for 'quality education' was narrowed down to social equations of power. The demand for preserving some higher educational institutions as 'centres of excellence' emanates from such a political position. Media education has not been able to distance itself from such polemical pedagogical claims, so far.

Theory as Skill

Media education at the post graduate level emphasises on providing 'skill' as well as 'knowledge'. The production skills in various media forms are provided and that remain the major focus. The 'knowledge' part has been occupied by normative theories and utopian positivist slogan of 'technology for development', media being merely reduced to 'technology'.

The concept of 'development' has been the contested terrain in India ever since Nehruvian state churned out its political mission. While being 'silent' on the ground realities that determined the cause and effect of development, the state-imagined technological experiments marked early media/communication studies, which continue even today in various manifestations of narratives of the state and market. Culture being the contested realm, these perceived pedagogical aspects masks not only the base but also the super structure, in a reverse Marxian model on society and culture.

Only a critical pedagogic approach could explore those contested realms. This should lead us to ponder over the need to imagine media education at the post graduate level to be more dense and laden with in-depth theoretical debates. At least students should be introduced pedagogically to various approaches and philosophical debates on media. The role of teacher being a facilitator, rather than a traditional *Guru*, whose autocratic 'cultural frustrations' used to define education.

The critique of Development Communication paradigms, emergence of Cultural Study as an inter-disciplinary approach and method, debates on information society and convergence media etc., have been some of the sites of expanded terrains which needs to be incorporated into media curricula. A look at the syllabus for UGC (NET) Lectureship in Mass Communication and Journalism will make us wonder how irresponsible one could be towards updating the syllabus prescribed for Journalism and Mass Communication teachers who, by virtue of it, become the creators of future media professional and researchers/academics of the country.

Today media is run without journalism[4] and therefore bowing down to the demands of the corporate would not serve the interests of democracy. The market may remain happy with a bunch of skilled glamorous journos who can churn out any saleable rubbish in the name of news. In order to create culturally sensitive, socially responsible and politically aware media professionals who could play a major role in democratisation of the country, the Universities as knowledge production centres should initiate the dialogue of social and cultural sensitivity, at least in their media schools.

A matured democracy needs responsible media persons, who are sensitive to cultural plurality, at the same time competent enough to handle the nuances of news both as product as well as socially, culturally constructed 'reality'. A re-look at our media education should be carried out in order to re-locate it in the context of global education. This exercise is of utmost important as many media schools tend to limit its horizon to the vested interests of some of the major media houses. In fact this may even result in the democratisation of newly emerged public sphere where counter-hegemonies of culture contest for fare share of resources.

References

1. See The Hindu, July 15, 2007. For a detailed reading of his historical take on Indian newspaper industry refer Eapen, K. E.

(1967). "Daily Newspapers in India: Their Status and Problems", Journalism Quarterly, Vol. 44, p. 52.

2. I am taking an Andersonian position of the construction of nation here. I am aware of the need of the critique of Anderson especially while referring nation in South Asian context. However, I would prefer to begin the discussion from Benedict Anderson's 'Imagined Communities' as the possibilities it brought forth has immense theoretical potential while addressing the issues on nation, community and media.

3. Robin Jeffrey has noted that in the 1970s, the American Society of Newspaper Editors [ASNE[set a goal that by the year 2000 American minorities would be represented in newsrooms in proportion to their numbers in the general population. That would have meant a total of twenty-six per cent minority representation, of which thirteen per cent would have been Black. The goal will not be met. In 1998, a survey in the *Columbia Journalism Review* found Blacks to account for 5.4 per cent of newspaper staffs; minorities, for 11.5 per cent.18 Nevertheless, major newspapers sought to recruit top Black journalists to satisfy affirmative-action targets, and American Blacks were publishers and managing editors of major publications across the United States. See Jeffrey, Robin (2001).

   '[NOT] being there: Dalits and India's newspapers', South Asia: Journal of South Asian Studies, 24:2, pp. 225-238.

4. See Sevanti, Ninan, "Media without Journalism", http://casi.ssc.upenn.edu//, 08.06.2007.

III. Media, Cricket Culture

11

Mapping Twenty-20 Cricket Culture

In the post-match ceremony of the Twenty-20 World Cup Cricket final held in South Africa recently, Shaoib Malik, the Pakistan captain thanked all Muslims across the world for supporting his team. This remark has irked many, who took no time in condemning the attempt to link religion with cricket as blasphemy against the game.

Incidentally, it was only a few months ago that Western media had portrayed the world cup team of Pakistan as a bunch of 'Islamic Fundamentalists', capable of doing anything even murdering their own coach. Perhaps, Shaoib Malik was addressing the political binaries constructed by Western media and global politics, at yet another altar of World Cup Cricket.

Muslim as 'Other' has been an accepted political vocabulary in the post 9/11 West and post-colonial/Hindu India. And so, Shaoib Malik's statement and its criticisms were quite expected, the political correctness of which cannot possibly be sought without contextualising it.

This article is neither an attempt to review Twenty-20 cricket, nor does it engage with the question of Islam and terrorism. My interest is to draw the unmarked, yet visible terrains of post-Mandal India by looking at the mirror image of the new version of cricket and its mass appeal.

And as such, Shaoib Malik's global Islam appeal assumes political dimension in the insurrected silence of Irfan Pathan. While the 'Global Other' in Shaoib Malik could asserted his identity by addressing a trans-national Muslim Community, 'national Other' in Irfan Pathan could not. Instead he had to prove his 'obedience' to the nation by adhering to the strict silencing of the secular/Hindu imagination.

Another possibility is that both are compelled to be 'obedient' within the dominant umbrella of respective national/religious identities and articulate accordingly. I would like to believe in this complex mesh of structurally overlapping identities and how human beings play within its confines.

The question that interests me is: How does it matter to the Indian camp (of nationalism), where a Muslim became 'Man of the Match' to help India clinch the title? Or does it matter at all? This question becomes relevant in the light of the indifference shown by Narendra Modi, Chief Minister of Gujarat and the state government towards Pathan brothers— Irfan and Yousuf. Modi has shown least interest in the victory while other state governments were competing with each other to announce rewards for the Twenty20 heroes from their respective states.

Modi was reported to have remarked that the match could have gone either side, hinting to underplay the brilliant performance of Irfan Pathan in the final. In fact, it was his 3-16 spell that has broken the strong batting line-up of Pakistan.

Though, Pakistan came back in the game, the young Indians kept their cool, bowled and fielded well pressurising the Pak batsmen, eventually wrapping up the match. The grant finale also turned out to be a face-saver for both the teams—India and Pakistan— particularly after the first round exit from ODI World Cup 2007 held in West Indies.

Counter-Culture of Mandalisation?

The way 'WE' deal with its 'Other' is pathetic and alarming. Pathan brothers are constituted in the Indian team as the patriotic 'secular' Muslim 'Other', devoid of Islamist identity, who serves the nation sincerely. This becomes possible by imagining Indian cricket team as the epitome of nationalism in the field, the nation being an *Hindu/brahmin* imagination.

It should be noted here that the whole imagination is male 'upper' caste *Hindu/brahmin.* Female counterparts of the game could hardly get the kind of euphoric welcome that the men's squad receives, as patriarchy does not recognise female as human.

Another angle to this conundrum could be drawn from the newspaper report that Karnataka Hockey players went on hunger strike in protest against the indifference shown by the state government. This happened at a time when whole country was hooked up to the victory procession of Twenty20 heroes in Mumbai.

Whereas the historical category of Dalit bahujan/minority-constituted sports and games such as Foot Ball, Hockey and Athletics were neglected, the male caste *Hindu/brahmin* dominated game like cricket receives accolades and money. The praxis of such configuration stems from the historical domination of *brahmins* over cricket. Theoretical base for it take roots in the materiality of caste-constituted gendered bodies.

S. Anand elaborates this aspect of cricket in the book *Brahmins & Cricket: Lagan's Millennial Purana and Other Myths* as: *"Cricket in India, especially the test variety, appears to be a game that has inherently suited the bodies and temperaments of the 'twice born."*

Ashis Nandy in *The Tao of Cricket* sites, *"cricket's touch of timelessness, its emphasis on purity, and its attempt to contain aggressive competition through ritualisation"* as reasons for the elitist choice of cricket. Ramachandra Guha, the cricket historian writes: *"Cricket being a non-body contact sport was certainly one attraction for the brahmin. Besides, to play this game you did not have to be physically very strong."*

These seminal works throw light on the brahminical engagement with the game right from the day they learnt the art and became 'native masters' succeeding the British coloniser. What happened in Indian nationalism followed suit in cricket as well. And both are celebrated with patriotic/nationalist fervour. The Indian state's appeasing of the male version of the game indicates this ideological praxis.

Over the years, cricket has expanded its reach and became accessible to the previously outcastes of the game—the Dalit bahujans. In fact, Boria Majumdar in his book *Twenty-Two Yards to Freedom,* while assessing the role cricket played in Indian national life, has argued that it acted as a means to cross class barriers and had a healthy following even outside the aristocracy and 'upper' middle classes well over a century ago.

Conquering the historical hurdles the post-colonial *shudra* has entered the *brahminical* realm of cricket and altered its structural hierarchy. It should be remembered that India became world cricket champions only twice—1983 ODI and 2007 twenty20— and both these occasions played under non-*brahmin* leadership—Kapil Dev and Mahendra Singh Dhoni respectively.

The place of *Dalits* in this whole culture of cricket is still not very different. They have to remain as the 'Other' of the 'Other' and mostly denied entry into the team. Guha points out: *"In a regional sense, it has democratised. But caste-wise, the composition of the team hardly reflects the diversity of our society. After Palwankar Baloo in the early part of the century, we haven't produced a single Dalit cricketer at the national level."* Palwankar Baloo could be part of the ODI format only, test cricket being the domain of *brahmins*.

Pathan's presence as 'Other' is essential to prove the 'secular' credentials of Indian polity, whereas *Dalits* could be denied it by invoking the brahminical philosophy of meritocracy. This is the paradox of secularism/nationalism and Mandalisation too. These aspects should make us look at post-colonial/Mandal Indian polity problematically. A critique of its brahminical orientation and subsequent disenchantment with the *Dalit* Question is warranted.

So, what if a Muslim child in Modi's Gujarat decides to play cricket in the name of Allah? Will our 'secularism' call him/her a 'communalist' again? Will the post-Mandal India and imagined/Mandalised counter-culture propose any paradigm shift in our thinking?

We need not wait till Shaoib Malik comes with the answer. It is time for us to seek answers. Are post-colonial *shudras* and *Dalits* also ready for the dialogue? These are larger questions that need to be answered in order to strengthen the process of democratisation of Indian polity. And thanks to Shaoib for throwing such a pertinent question to the national Indian mindset.

12

Media Spectacle and the New 'Other'

There is another dimension to the culture of cricket that could be drawn from the unprecedented growth of Television Channels. The social and cultural impact of this phenomenon has constituted, to a greater extent, for the popularity of cricket in the country.

The political economy of cricket and television industry share similar materialistic ground and revolves around the philosophy of spectacle. Bourdieu's observation on the spectacle of Olympics is relevant here. For him, Olympics is "doubly hidden" in the "ensemble of representations" of media spectacle. "*...no one sees all of it, and no one sees that they don't see it. Every television viewer can have the illusion of seeing the (real) Olympics.*" And it is this element of spectacle and its possibility that attract television industry to cricket. Cricket culture, therefore, owes much to the "ensemble of media representations".

Though Bourdieu looks at 'media spectacle' as the domination of television over other mediums that mediate power equations, I do not share his anxieties.

Twenty-20 cricket, the 'Other' of classical test cricket and shortest of the shorter version of the game, has heralded a new era in the history of world cricket. Encompassing all possible *masalas* of a three and half hour long Bollywood blockbuster, the fineness and precision of Tennis and Golf, the twists and turns of a Soccer shoot-out; the power strokes of Baseball; glamour of Basketball with its dancing girls- the game has attracted a new bunch of fans as well. And it has offered another spectacle for television, favourite cool medium of Canadian media theoretician Marshal McLuhan, which carries with it the massaging message for the masses.

The format of this new version of cricket has also created a 'Twenty20 Other'— Sachin, Dravid and Ganguly. The brahmin *trio* who had to shun the classical style of cricket (which suits the brahminical body and vigor) to win laurels in ODI format, now see themselves at the altar of rejection by the masses.

The masses who invented *Galli Cricket* constitute a significant factor in configuring the new format and stars of the game. As Jeff Boycott told to BBC, *"The game is short, sweet and great fun; it brings new people into contact with cricket."* Rohit Brijnath (*Sportstar*) puts it as, *"... We [masses] played Twenty20 before it was invented."*

Dhoni, the present Indian Twenty20 and ODI cricket captain hails from Jharkhand, a predominantly non-cricket playing state. Dhoni's remark that *"players from small towns learn the art of the game in the hard way"*, points towards the socio-cultural dimensions of cricket and its transformation in the light of diversification of societal power relations. Pathans and Dhonis are the product of such transformation.

However the entry of *shudra/non-brahmin* into the brahminical realm of cricket has not changed the ideological mindset of the game and its star players. They eulogise 'Test Cricket' and keep a secret romantic dream of ensuring a birth in the test squad, thereby succumbing to the classical/brahminical imagination of the game. (See, Yuvraj clamouring for a birth in the test squad.) Thus, the puritanical imaginations of cricket chain Twenty20 also to the narrow brahminical confines.

So, what does Shaoib Malik's appeal mean to us, Indians? Does it mock at our 'victory'? And then, who is the 'real' winner of Twenty20 cricket? The victorious young Indian team; the masses who invented *Galli Cricket*; or the brahmin trio who did not play Twenty20? Perhaps, the answer to this would be a pointer towards the diversification of Indian cricket and its future heroes.

13

Vinod Kambli: Experiments with Caste and Willow

Indian newspapers reported that Vinod Kambli, the Indian cricketer during the shooting of a television show had vehemently attacked BCCI for discriminating against him based his caste and skin colour and criticised his childhood friend Sachin Tendulkar for being less 'friendly' at his bad times. Though, Kambli has denied these reports later, the author shares the 'Kambli Moment' in his life that point towards the caste factor in cricket and life.

Kambli, I knew it years ago. Perhaps you didn't. Or what else kept you silent for long? I know, cricket like brahmanism is a mythical institution that will lead one to the illusion of empowered self. But, I expected you to throw it back with the same ease with which you pick up and throw to get your opponent run out. And how can I forget your beautiful smile; the mumbling after a diving effort to save a single; the naughty grin after an effortless catch; the languishing return from the crease and the enigmatic flow of energy in the field with the usual encouraging words to fellow players. How can I forget you Kambli, though you were not my role model? Nor Sachin was. Never ever.

I was a 12-13 years old right handed batsman and medium pace bowler mesmerised completely by the legendary Kapil Dev and carried away by the genius of the then young Mohammad Azharuddin. I can still play that leg glance and flick with much ease, but not as elegant and perfect as Azhar. I was initiated into cricket by my sports-loving father, who because of his passion for sports named me 'Ranjit' (may be after great Ranjit Singhji or some Punjabi sportsman).

It was mid-1980s and we had yet to get a television set at home. During cricket season, my brother and me used to go to a nearby Nair family to watch cricket along with other caste Hindu friends. The Nair lady in the house also loved cricket and she used to watch cricket with us. It was during one such occasion that I first saw you playing. Frankly, I was not attracted to your left-handed batting. In fact I was never attracted to any left handed batsman except Syed Anvar of Pakistan, (and later of course, the legendary Brian Lara),but that is an altogether different story.

I saw a glow in your eyes and thought, like in your world record-breaking partnership with Sachin for your school team, one day you will create history for us. I always wanted you to be ahead (don't know why?). I liked your style and enthusiasm in the field; your dark complexion had a peculiar charm that even now reminds me of my late father. But I never knew about your caste and that it can decide one's future.

It was during one of those television viewing sessions that one day the Nair lady pointing at your television image remarked; "how can this black—be in Indian team?" (writing from my childhood memory) And all my friends laughed. My admiration for you fumed at that moment. I sat wonderstruck silently listening to the humiliating remarks about you.

I never knew then that it could be your caste status and skin colour that made the Nair lady makes such rude and casteist remarks. I could sense some hidden meaning in the remarks and the response of my caste Hindu friends, but could not express it. I felt as though some one had hit me with a willow just below my chest. I could see the moment of desperation that you had displayed at this late hour in you then itself. Weren't you aware of it? Whether you knew it or not, but the world has made you a history-sheeter out of your caste, skin colour and your own unique style.

Kambli, you may not be a great success, but you are not a failure. Your war has just begun. May be, you came bit early. The missions will be accomplished, but not as you and me, but as new we. Take your willow and wear your gloves. Every innings will comes has started again. Just wait for your turn. Good luck!

Bibliography

Adorno, Theodor W. 2001. *The Culture Industry: Selected Essays on Mass Culture*, New York: Routledge

Aloysius, G. 2003. *Nationalism without a Nation in India,* New Delhi: Oxford University Press

Althusser, Louis. 1971. *Ideology and Ideological State Apparatuses. Lenin and Philosophy. Monthly Review Press*, New York, pp. 127-86

Anand, S. 2003. *Brahmans and Cricket Lagaan's millennial purana and other myths,* Chennai—Navayana

Anand, S. 2005. *Visible Dalit Invisible Brahmin, in Practising Journalism: Values, Constraints, Implication*, ed. Rajan, Nalini. pp. 172-197. New Delhi: Sage Publications

Anderson, Benedict. 1983. *Imagined Communities: Reflection on the Origin and Spread of Nationalism*, London/Verso Editions

Bourdieu, Pierre.1998. *On Television and Journalism* London: Pluto Press

Majumdar, Boria. 2004. *Twenty-Two Yards to Freedom: A Social History of Indian Cricket,* Delhi: Penguine Books

Nandy, Ashish. 2002. *The Tao of Cricket On games of destiny and the destiny of games,* New Delhi: Oxford University Press

Carey, James W. 2009 (1989). *Communication as Culture*, London: Routledge

Chomsky, Noam and Herman, Edward S. 2008. *A Propaganda Model in Journalism: Critical Concepts in Media and Cultural Studies Vol 2*, ed. Howard Tumber, pp. 85-123. London: Routledge

Collins, Richard et al. 1986. *Media, Culture and Society*, New Delhi: Sage Publications

Campbell, Kate. ed. 2004. *Journalism, Literature and Modernity: From Hazlitt to Modernism*. Edinburgh: Edinburgh University Press

Conboy, Martin. 2002. *The Press and Popular Culture*, New Delhi: Sage Publications

Curran, James et. al. 1986. *Media, Culture and Society A Critical Reader*, New Delhi: Sage Publications

Deuz, Mark. 2005. *What is Journalism?: Professional identity and ideology of journalists reconsidered, Journalism*, Vol. 6(4)

Eapen, K. E. 1967. *Daily Newspapers in India: Their Status and Problems', Journalism Quarterly*. Vol. 44, p. 52

Eisenstein, Elizabeth L. 1986. *On revolution and the printed word, Revolution in History*, Porter, R and Teich, M, pp. 186-205. OUP: Cambridge

Ferguson, Robert. 2004. *Media in Question*, London: Arnold

Gupta, Charu. ed. 2012. *Gendering Colonial India: Reform, Print, Caste and Communalism*, New Delhi: Orient Black Swan

Gupta, Uma Das. 1977. The Indian Press 1870-1880: *A Small World of Journalism, Modern Asian Studies*, II, 2, pp. 213-235

Gurevitch, Michael et al. ed. 1982. *Culture, Society, and the Media*, London: Routledge

Guru, Gopal. 2002. *How Egalitarian are Social Sciences in India?, Economic and Political Weekly*, December 14, pp. 5003-5009

Habermass, Jürgen. 1991. *The Structural Transformation of the Public Sphere: An Inquiry into a Category of Bourgeois Society*. Massachusetts: the MIT Press

Hanitzsch, Thomas. 2007. *Deconstructing Journalism Culture: Toward a Universal Theory, Communication Theory*, Vol. 17, Number 4, November, pp. 367-385

Hardtmann, Eva-Maria. 2009. *The Dalit Movement in India: Local Practices, Global Connections*. New Delhi: Oxford University Press

Hassan, Zoya. ed. 2000. *Politics and the State in India: Readings in Indian Government and Politics-3* New Delhi: Sage

Innis, Harold A.1942. *The Newspaper in economic development, The Journal of Economic History*, Vol. 2, Supplement: The Tasks of Economic History, December, pp. 1-33

Jensen, Klaus Bruhn. ed. 2002. *A Handbook of Media and Communication Research–Quantitative and Qualitative Methodologies*. London: Routledge

Keeble, Richard, ed. 2005. *Print Journalism: A Critical Introduction*, London: Routledge

Louw, Eric P. 2001. *The Media and Cultural Production*. New Delhi: Sage Publications

McLuhan, Marshall. 1964. *Understanding Media: The Extensions of Man*. London: Routledge & Kegan Paul Limited

Murthy, Ramachandra K. 2003. *Rural Reporting in India*. Hyderabad: Prajasakti Book House

Parenti, Michael.1986. *Inventing Reality: The Politics of the Mass Media*. New York: St. Martin's Press

Prasad, Chandrabhan. 2004. *Dalit Diary 1999-2003 Reflections on Apartheid in India*. Chennai: Navayana

Rajagopal, Aravind. 2001. *Politics after Television: Hindu Nationalism and the Reshaping of the Public in India.* UK: Cambridge University Press

Thirumal, P. 1997. *State media and national culture in Communication and Culture: New Perspectives and Applications.* ed. Dua M. R. and Manonmani, T., pp. 10-13, New Delhi: Galgotia Publishing Company

Tuchman, Gaye. 1978. *Making News: A Study in the Construction of Reality*, New York: Free Press

Wilson II, Clint C.1985. Gutiérrez, Félix,*Minorities and Media – Diversity and The End of Mass Communication.* New Delhi: Sage Publications.

Index

U